Words
on
Troubled Waters

Published by Lutra River Press

Llandysul, Wales 2024
ISBN 978-1-7385126-0-7

Printed in the UK on unbleached recycled paper
and card using eco-friendly ink

Edited by Simone Mansell Broome

Words
on
Troubled Waters

Ten writers from Wales responding to the environmental decline of Afon Teifi. Their words were displayed and heard as part of the **'Art on Troubled Waters'** exhibition in the **Seagull Gallery**, Cardigan, at the mouth of the Teifi.

Art
on
Troubled Waters

was a multi-media Afon Teifi-related exhibition curated by Lou Weldon for The Seagull Gallery in the autumn of 2023. This was a labour of love highlighting the beauty and the pollution of a major Welsh river. It included work from local artists, photographers, glass makers, musicians, potters, but it also featured the words of local writers.

'Words on Troubled Waters' has gathered these written pieces (mostly poems) together. Their message is clear and stark.

Afon Teifi was quoted, in 2023, as being the ninth most polluted river in the UK. The Seagull's exhibition highlighted concerns about the river's decline, to raise awareness of Afon Teifi's plight.

The Seagull
Y Gwylan
Cardigan

In February 2022, trained designer Lou Weldon opened The Seagull Gallery. She wanted to show local work from all mediums and offer an intimate gallery experience with more artist involvement. Louise was also motivated, not only by aesthetics, but also by a desire to further public engagement with critical concerns including women's issues, climate crisis and the environment. There have been two major environment focussed exhibitions so far:

'Changing Times', an artist's response to climate change, 2022
and
'Art on Troubled Waters', 2023

In 2024 the gallery will be for hire to be taken over by artists, poets, potters, glassmakers, printers, writers, etc. A completely artist-led gallery in the centre of Cardigan.

info@seagullcardigan.co.uk 07810 254853
Facebook – The Seagull
Instagram – theseagull21

Contents

River Talk	Kathy Miles	9
This River was called Teifi before the Romans came	Sue Moules	10
Canoeing on the Teifi	Amanda Pickering	11
An Elegy, a Song	Simone Mansell Broome	12
A Working Life	Ann Jay	18
We are Water	Jane Campbell	19
Excerpts	Josie Smith	20
Poem in which i go to a meeting in the village hall with representatives from Dwr Cymru	Kittie Belltree	22
Cynefin	Julia Angell	24
The Broken Cup	Julia Angell	25
Kingfisher's mirror	Jackie Biggs	26
Not you, not me, not us	Jackie Biggs	28

River-Talk

Otter spraint is scribbled onto stone
like Ogham script. Trees lean towards the river

as if to catch a whisper from the shallows; curlew
and lapwing dip beaks among the reed beds.

A demoiselle, gleaming malachite, lands
on a leaf, dainty as a tiny ballerina.

From mountains to the estuary, it flows through
bog and ford, towns where concrete blooms

in ruined buildings, traffic sings at dawn, sirens
feral the night to wake us from our dreaming.

But here, where water rushes over boulders,
the heron slips quietly into a hunch of sleep,

and salmon jump, each time a leap of faith; haul
of gut and muscle, fins shimmering like wings.

Driven by a memory, they shift from sea to stream,
knowing from birth there will be this return;

the way that we, too, swim against the current,
gravity pulling us down to still green pools,

but always with the impulse to scale impossible
heights, fighting to get back to where we started.

Kathy Miles

This River was called Teifi before the Romans came

Teifi sings the river as it journeys to the sea,

teifiteifiteifi, teifiteifiteifi, teifiteifiteifi

as it glugs and splashes into waterfalls,

jumps across air to land and move on

calling *teifiteifiteifi,teifiteifiteifi,*

as it makes its way into a broader

muscle of water voyaging across borders

on its 112 kilometres or 76 miles

wriggling through land taking twigs, branches,

shopping trolleys, slurry, old shoes

through sheep grazing pasture

where kingfishers dip in a moment of turquoise,

herons perch in their grey cloaks,

salmon rise,

insects bicker in sunlight.

Teifi croons the river as it slinks through day and night

seeing things it can't tell

TeifiTeifiTeifi,

it sings its song of ancient name

as it chants and shimmies round corners

where otters play.

Sue Moules

Canoeing on the Teifi

Between trees the blue-green flicker
of a damselfly, the splash of a fish.

We have paddled the Teifi in all its moods,
balanced on the swollen muscle of its trunk after rain,

felt the muddy rush of its current push
against the bow as we struggle back up-river.

Have witnessed too, oak roots cradling drowned sheep,
alder, willow, snared by twine, silage wrap, plastic bottles.

Lately, I have seen slurry slosh through a woodland
stream, all scum and bubble, splashing anemone and fern

as it slipped into the river; water where I've watched
otters frolic, sleek as the sheen on the river's evening skin.

Water, where I've heard children run in-and-out, laughter,
the plonk of pebbles, wet dogs, families picnicking on the banks,

and old couples hand-in-hand paddling in the shallows.
I remember too, us sliding down a June river, the fishermen

in their caves of leaves, hooked by the stillness of sky
held in a mirror of water, the scent of balsam, brine,

a leaf brushing silence.

Amanda Pickering

An Elegy, a Song

I am witch of the old tales, the Welsh tales,
all stories, tall tales and fairytales.
I am vengeance, jealousy, quick to rage,
slow, if ever, to forgive. You may try
to escape my wrath, to flee punishment,
to cheat death, hide in plain sight, use disguise,
or forms could change as a challenge, a test.
Prey or predator, we work our wiles. Know.
These stones, these hills, these trees, this water,
they hold my memories. I always win.

Wrong river…you know the story. I gave
that lad, that disobedient boy, such
a simple task. Watch the cauldron; don't taste;
don't touch. Humans get tempted, give in,
fail. Despite my powers, the seed grew.
I was woman too and gave birth. Taliesin.
I tried to destroy him but he came back,
rescued in the fisherman's catch of salmon.
From our shapeshifting duel, our battle of wits,
from the servant's defeat, from chaos
and cruelty, came good. The prophet, the bard.

April can green the land, bring birth, is not always
the cruellest month. New life arrives
and sometimes is not swallowed, drowned
by spring rains. The young can survive.

We put up statues to dead men, (some women too,
but not enough). Brave men, rich men, strong men,
men who made some mark, whatever sort,
however ill or well it chimes, now, with us.

But the otter? A gift to the town
of Cardigan, Aberteifi, in '88,
fiftieth birthday of Dyfed's Wildlife Trust.
He stands by the bridge, symbol of survival,
revival, the creature's return, even though fragile:
Lutra lutra doing well in many rivers,
less so here.

We've always fought for space,
species against species, need against need,
greed against greed. The scales have tipped so far
to what we think's our favour: there are
so many weapons in our arsenal.

Just half a century since we stopped hunting otters.
We thought of them like foxes, vermin, pests
to be culled. Surely it was our birthright
to kill, uncontested by *Lutra lutra*,
this semi-aquatic mammal. There was
Coracle fishing on the Teifi, boosting
the incomes of the ordinary man,
farm workers, quarrymen. It helped them thrive.
Just as country folk poached from the landowner,
accepted quietly - until a man was caught.

Coracle fishing spawned a craft, a culture
all its own, quaint, arcane, traditional,
an enterprise for visitors to gawp at,
admire, digging deep for coins and notes,
tidy sums for the locals.

On sunny days, by Cenarth Bridge, a man
sets up his stall on a picnic bench, lays out
his catch of books, sells stories - times when
the river teemed with fish, with no end in sight.

He rowed across the channel, Kent to France,
in '73, in a coracle. I bought his books.

Visitors fill the carpark, marvel at the falls,
read about those men in crazy, hand-built craft,
salmon leaping. Nothing much to see now
but an oily film on the surface, thick scum
around the rocks. There'll be no paddling today.
And I'm told of friends' children, stomach bugs
after river swimming. Coincidence perhaps.

Access for all is the goal, a decking boardwalk
beside the river, a citizen's right. Now the deck
is blighted with dog shit. It will go soon
anyhow, washed by rain into the Teifi,
or taken home in the tread of trainers, tyres
of wheelchairs, toddlers' buggies.

I talk to a mother, here since the eighties,
who's often picnicked, never stopped her kids
from swimming. She remembers fewer people,
fewer tourists, no new developments,
and the fishing was *epic,* the stuff of legend,
pub regaling, fading photos. This mother
is on her way to the pool, feels it's safer now.

I speak to walkers, visiting for eleven years,
never seen dipper, otter, heron, kingfisher,
not one salmon, just rubbish, and that dog mess.

My friend, who left ten years back, recalls much fishing,
mostly with rod and line, children paddling,
otters, swans, a splash of colour
from the kingfisher, how one day,
from her Cardigan townhouse window,

she counted twenty swans, (bevy, flock or herd,
as on the water), and she cried.

I read that last year there were about
14,000 hours of overflow into the river. It sounds
quite nice until you click what it is that's flowing.
And how were those folk we entrust with duties
watery, how were they rewarded
for their skills, diligence, crimes?
Salmon and sea trout need clean water.

I chat with neighbours who moved here in '06
for a better kind of living, less traffic,
cleaner air, clearer skies, a slower pace.
Their land is bordered by a Teifi stream. Sea trout,
brown trout once filled their Nant. Dippers flew in
each day. Grey wagtails came in spring.
He gathered branches, laid them across the stream,
fashioning perch, launch pad, vantage point
for their frequent kingfisher guest.
All declined slowly, steadily. Brown trout
still sometimes spawn but their young die.
Their food has gone.

On some evenings you might hear
an otter family down by the bridge,
but they're a rare, precious sight. A few young males
turn up in spring, move around the pools
on neighbouring land, take their fill of frogs
and toads, then go. **This is no place
to build your holt, raise your family.**
He says the water mostly looks the same, but…
fly life's reduced. All life's reduced. The cycle's broken.
Impacts ripple out and some are not yet known.
He mourns what's lost.

But humans too need homes. People want houses
by the river. Why not? The sight and sound
of water moving, whether it's *vital*,
whether it's *barren* - we barely know or care -
it restores, soothes, heals, touches the human heart.
We felled trees, cleared scrub, made riverside paths
for man on foot or cycle, but the otter loses -
secure habitat, sleeping quarters. We make our nests
in lovely places. Of course there's talk
of phosphates, flooding

but money talks louder, and money's power
and power always sings. Maybe a token scuffle
with the planners but the plan of the rich man
is bound to win. And he'll laud the benefits
*his schemes will bring **to all**, to tourism,*
cash-strapped home-hunters, incomers
and the economy alike. Everyone's a winner;
there'll be a conservation gain. So, some of this
is true, and all of this will make him richer too.

Gwion Bach became a rabbit, then Ceridwen
a dog. Gwion a fish, and Ceridwen an otter, Gwion
a bird, Ceridwen a hawk, Gwion a grain of corn
and Ceridwen the hen who ate that grain of corn.
Shapeshifting stories show the circle. **We see it**
but don't like it, sitting as it does
in an awkward, prickly place. We need our nature
pretty, or useful, or both. Red in tooth and claw
gets tricky when it's close. We can point the finger,
but we, like Gwion, failed to do a basic task.

If the river survives so will the otter
We need the whole picture, not Taliesin,
not self-interest, not blinkered greed,

not blind optimism. We've lost our balance,
the balance, the patterns behind everything.

I am witch of the old tales, the Welsh tales,
all stories, tall tales and fairytales.
Prey or predator, we work our wiles. Know.
These stones, these hills, these trees, this water,
this river,
they hold my memories.

Simone Mansell Broome

A Working Life

It's all about the bridges,
        if your patch is the Teifi valley.
You need to know where they are
        when you meet the river every day.
                You learn its moods.
        Sometimes it's a trickle,
other times it boils.

Journeys are not long.
        You never get to Poppit or Cors Caron,
    rarely to Lampeter or Cardigan.
Llandysul is home,
            Henllan, Llanybydder, Llechryd,
    Newcastle Emlyn, well known.

        You'd pause at Cenarth,
            for a look at the falls,
    imagine salmon leaping,
                men in coracles.
Afternoons off you'll play Pooh sticks with the children
                at Alltcafan.
    Just once you saw the turquoise flash of a kingfisher there.

            Back and forth you go,
                day after day, week after week,
        past farms and villages,
            castles and woollen mills
        compiling a map,
    making connections.
        You discover the crossings,
                the people, the stories
woven around a single silver thread,
            yr afon Teifi.

Ann Jay

- 18 -

We are Water

Sea lies on her bed
longing to soar.
She begs rough winds
to hurl her high
but the weight of her waves
stop her reaching the arching sky.
Then one hot summer night a tingle
draws her into droplets
of dragon's breath
light as fluff
and the morning sun can scoop her up.
As a cloud she scuds over land and sea
belonging to nobody.
Cloud watches the whole world
from on high
until, being airy
becomes sort of lonely.
Cloud longs to feel connected,
slide her skin over mossy stones.
She seeks out the tallest mountains
lies alongside their sharpest peaks to weep,
and gravity's magic brings release,
thunders her down,
raining into river,
streaming and laughing,
roiling muddy around the bends.
Water dances so fast
that land sails past.
Within days she has flooded home,
always restored to
ceaseless sea.

Jane Campbell

Excerpts

Excerpt from Diary of a Shielding Yogini
ISBN 978-1-908146-07-6
Chapter Four
June 2020

June 1ˢᵗ - We join Stella and Alisha on the banks of the River Teifi in Lampeter and we all swim!!!

Wow! The water feels sublime, almost warm, not exactly bathtub warm, but definitely not freeze your socks off cold. And the longer I am in the water the warmer it feels. We have a deep waterhole about five metres long and four metres wide. Plenty big enough to swim up and down.

I like swimming upstream best, as I can see the sunlight playing in the trees and it is heart-achingly beautiful. There is nothing in the world like swimming in the open air. I always swim backstroke, I love being able to look at the sky while swimming, and I don't like the feeling of my face in water, some subliminal fear of drowning, I think.

When I stand, water up to my chest, Alisha gives me another air-hug, and I hug her back. Stella and Alisha have been swimming in the river every day recently.

"We could have a real hug, Nana," she says, smiling her funny, wrinkly-face smile at me. I am tempted. She can see that. Every time we are together, we edge closer and closer to one another.

"It will be safe," she says, blue eyes sparkling at me. "We'll be underwater so no virus can get us. And we can hold our breath."

She looks adorable and I am convinced.

We breathe in deeply, hold our breath, turn our heads away from one another and hug. To feel her in my arms again, at last, is like holding heaven. I cradle the back of her head in my hand and melt into her, as she melts into me. We pull apart, and beam at one another. "Shall we do it again?" She asks.

We breathe in deeply and move together again. Smudger and Stella look over at us. There is enough love in this little pool of the Teifi to fill the universe.

Alisha hugs Smudger too.

We swim some more, clamber out, and dress. Nobody shivers. It is seven o'clock in the evening and still really warm. I wish this weather would last forever.

Excerpt from Cambrian News 11/04/2023
REVEALED: Map shows which stretches of River Teifi saw most sewage pollution last year
https://www.cambrian-news.co.uk/news/environment/revealed-map-shows-which-stretches-of-river-teifi-saw-most-sewage-pollution-last-year-606404

The Teifi saw the sixth highest level of sewage pollution of any river in England and Wales last year – and a new map has revealed on which stretches spills were most common.

Data released last week from the country's primary water supplier Dŵr Cymru and environmental regulator Natural Resources Wales (NRW) revealed a concerning record of discharges across seas, rivers and waterways in Ceredigion last year.

An analysis of the data estimates the county saw more than 3,800 dumps last year – equating to a total duration of 33,000 hours or about four years of overflow.

Josie Smith

Poem in which i go to a meeting in the village hall with representatives from Dwr Cymru

well it was meant to be
a meeting
but really it was a shit show
you know because while i was
there i learned about such things as
licensed sewer overflows
or
the power to dump shit and run
the power to dump shit run
and make the customer pay later
although i thought i'd already paid
which is why
i came to this meeting because
i wanted to ask why
every time it rains my house stinks of shit
of shit why every time it rains the water
companies spill more shit
spill more shit from mouths more shit
ending up in the mouth
of the river
i mean isn't it time to end this shit this shitty
shit system of self-monitored sewage discharge
in which shit is considered to be a low impact issue
i mean surely the impact
of shit is shit
wherever you're standing
sitting or shitting its shit
sitting on arse ache chairs in the village hall
i didn't want to come tonight
because life's pretty shit right now
i mean i'm swimming in it
every time it rains its

a shower of shit
every time it rains it's a corporate shower
of cash in exchange
for slurry plastic and a cocktail of chemicals spewing
this shit storm into the river mouth
while the regulators plie us with
PowerPoint presentations and pie charts
it was meant to be a meeting
but really it was more like
a mouthful a manifesto
for a network of crumbling pumping stations
and sewage pipes that leak and spill
and mouths
full of shit
just
waiting
to happen

Kittie Belltree

Cynefin

We spread beyond borders, arteries flowing
pulsing outwards over years, searching
for the heart place, for hiraeth.
And where the Teifi hugs the sea
we meet. We talk of belonging, compare
our bones, our height, our likes
three cousins, sixty years on.
In Celtic lands the cliffs and inlets echo,
we shout from the Blessing Stone, *SHWMAE*
hear her call us back.
Tales blown as a cliff top crow, come to rest
on these cloud dappled shores.
Button mouth they called my mum – we compare
smiles. And they tell me our great great grandmother
came from Pembrokeshire, as my finger traces
the maternal line, all the way back home.

Julia Angell

The Broken Cup

You stand, feet sinking into filthy silt
gasping on the stench of foreshore, eyes drawn
to past times, pieces of broken china

the bent blue bough of the willow that leant
across the flow finally cracked, turned the tide
into tears that fell dull as a lifeless body

you want to piece it back together, to grasp
the cup once more, hold it as if there was never
anything so precious as steaming tea

but it can no longer quench your thirst
cannot offer you life
this cup – it was in the palm of your hand.

Julia Angell

Kingfisher's mirror
(at Cilgerran Gorge)

Kingfisher's blue, a rapid shimmer
shoots over watery mirror,
his dart piercing a reverie.
My mind travels back, many millennia,
reflecting how ice age meltwater cut new river channels,
forced up hill under gigantic ice sheets,
making new courses.
The power of that.

Back nine hundred years,
to wonder how they worked the slate
and carried it away to make the great walls
of the castle down the river.

From one-hundred years ago, hear the shouts of men,
the clank of shovels on stone, chisels cracking slate.
Know the scent of ceaseless dust, persistent damp.
Hundreds of men labouring high across sheer cliffs,
spiders on pale walls.
Boats coming up on the tide to carry slate to all the world,
from here – this quiet place.
Spoil silts up the river, changes this landscape.

When daily work stopped here
men went to war, quarries went to ruin –
and back to nature.
Banks of slate still slip sometimes
into cool running waters.
But walls of rock stand ever silent
in the steep of the gorge.

Sounds of the river, ever changing,
yet never ceasing, bring you back to now.
Water slipping over pebbles, rapids shoot,
rocking stones, in the wide sunshine flows,
light carried on steady currents.

Now trees find life here, roots among rock,
lichens mingle with mosses;
scent of spring gorse, birds twitter.
Here otters play, falcons hunt, salmon leap,
and kingfishers shimmer over mirrors of time.

Jackie Biggs

Not you, not me, not us

It's not just the Teifi...
The principal tributaries of the Teifi
are referenced here from source to sea.

Afon Mwyro, Nant Glasffrwd, Afon Meurig,
      stickleback, beetle larvae, water crowfoot
           phosphorous, plastic coffee cups, slurry.

Afon Fflur, Camddwr Fach, Camddwr,
      eel, water shrew, owl
           pipe breaches, domestic cleaning products

Brennig, Nant Carfan, Afon Brefi,
      lamprey, frogspawn, kingfisher
           sewage, chemicals, road run-off

           not me, not you, not us

Nant Digonest, Nant Clywedog, Ffrwd Cynon,
      barbel, water vole, minnow
           leaking septic tanks, fly-tipping, wetwipes

Nant Gou, Nant Dulas, Nant Hathren,
      brown trout, water fleas, willow
           sewage, nitrates, airborne emissions

Nant Eiddig, Nant y Gwragedd, Nant Dolgwm,
      grayling, otter, pondskaters
           animal waste, leaking pipes, chemicals

           not me, not you, not us

Afon Granell, Afon Duar, Nant Hust,
  sewin, water nymph, heron
    muck spreading, insecticides, cosmetics

Nant Ceiliog, Nant Caradog, Nant Cwm-du,
  bream, bats, butterflies
    sweet wrappers, drink cans, leaking septic tanks

Nant Cledlyn, Nant Fylchog, Afon Clettwr,
  salmon, kingfisher, dragonflies
    sewage, rain run-off, phosphorous

          not me, not you, not us
          It's all of us

Nant Wern-macwydd, Gwenffrwd, Afon Cerdin,
  shrimp, dipper, flatworms
    plastic water bottles, airborne pollutants, slurry

Afon Tyweli, Nant Merwydd, Hoffnant,
  bream, alder, pine marten
    phosphorous, chemicals, broken pipes

Afon Gwr-fach, Afon Siedi, Camnant,
  salmon, otter, eel
    sewage, silage wrap, road run-off

          not me, not you, not us

Nant Bachnog, Nant Iago, Nant Bargoed,
  stickleback, beetle larvae, heron
    phosphorous, sandwich wrappers, fly-tipping

Afon Cynllo, Afon Cwm-wern, Nant Halen,
    lamprey, water voles, dippers
        road run-off, sewage, wetwipes

Afon Arad, Nant Sarah, Afon Ceri,
    barbel, minnow, badger
        leaking septic tanks, muck spreading

        not me, not you, not us

Afon Nawmor, Afon Hirwaun, Afon Cych,
    salmon, otter, eel
        sewage, chemicals, road run-off

Afon Eifed, Nant Arberth, Afon Morgenau,
    bream, bats, butterflies
        cling film, cigarette butts, leaking septic tanks

Afon Plysgog, Nant Rhyd-y-fuwch, Afon Piliau,
    brown trout, damselflies, willow
        sewage, herbicides, airborne emissions

Afon Mwldan, Nant Degwen, Nant-y-ferwig
    shrimp, lamprey, kingfisher
        muck-spreading, plastics, milk cartons

        *it's me, it's you, **it's all of us.***

Jackie Biggs

The contributors

Kathy Miles' work has appeared widely in magazines and anthologies. Her fourth full collection of poetry, Bone House, was published by Indigo Dreams in 2020.

Sue Moules is published in New Welsh Review, Planet, Poetry Wales, Ambit, and in anthologies including Poetry Wales 25 Years (Seren), Sixty Poems for Haiti (Cane Arrow Press), Glimmer Anthology (Cinnamon Press) . Her latest collection is The Moth Box (Parthian)

Amanda Pickering is an artist and poet living near Lampeter. Her creative inspiration comes from walking her dog in the surrounding countryside. Her poems have appeared in The Grapevine and in the last three anthologies of Lampeter Writers' Workshop. She is also a member of The Poetry Matters Collective who launched their first pamphlet in 2023.

Simone Mansell Broome is a Welsh-born published writer of poetry, prose and children's fiction. She's passionate about the environment. Simone's read on BBC radio and been commissioned by both ITV and local venues, including three poems for **The Seagull Gallery**. www.simonemansellbroome.com.

Ann Jay has twice been placed in the Hippocrates Prize and was commended in 2021. Her work has appeared in Spelt magazine and on the Wildfire Words website. One of her poems was incorporated into a quilt by Judy Fairless and exhibited in England and Wales. She was recently commended in the Trio Uganda prize.

Jane Campbell: Winner of the Geoff Stevens Memorial Poetry Prize, her first collection, *Slowly as Clouds,* is published by Indigo Dreams. www.indigodreamspublishing.com/jane-campbell. Jane also won the Disability Arts Cymru Creative Writing Award in 2022. Her work has appeared in magazines & anthologies. Her poem 'The Gardener' was featured in a BBC Wales programme 'Giants in the Sky'.

Josie Smith loves the wildness and beauty of West Wales, which she often celebrates in her prose and poetry. Her recent publications include Tamboura (Cowry 2023) and Diary of a Shielding Yogini (Cowry 2021.) She is a member of the Lampeter Writer's Workshop and has an MA in Creative Writing. Email tambourathebook@gmail.com

Dr Kittie Belltree's debut poetry collection Sliced Tongue and Pearl Cufflinks is published by Parthian (2019). Her poems, short fiction and reviews have appeared in numerous journals and anthologies, and she has just completed her first novel.

Julia (Jules) Angell gives Walks with Words in and around St Dogmaels - where the Teifi meets the sea. She is finishing her Creative Writing MA having been awarded a Post Graduate Diploma with Distinction from Lampeter in Spring 2023. She has been published online and in print and is currently compiling her first collection.

Jackie Biggs is co-organiser of Cardigan's monthly Cellar Bards spoken word event. She's had three collections of poetry published. Her work appears in many anthologies. She is currently working on a series of poems related to climate crisis. Her poetry blog is:- http://jackie-news.blogspot.co.uk

Thanks

—to those who campaign on behalf of the River Teifi, especially mentioning the Save The Teifi / Achubwch Y Teifi group. www.teifi.one

-to Lou Weldon and The Seagull Gallery, for curating and hosting the 'Art on Troubled Waters' exhibition and associated performances in Autumn 2023

-to all the poets

-to the folk at the Mulberry Bush, Lampeter for making sure the exhibition and the poetry continue to be seen and heard in 2024

-to Jackie, Kay and Roger for helping to put this book together

-and to **Ann Fletcher-Williams** for allowing the use of her pieces 'Journey's end' and 'Salmon leap' both exhibited in 'Art on Troubled Waters'. Ann is a painter living in Cardigan. Her work is about belonging and her relationship with the hills, coastlines, seascapes and rivers of Pembrokeshire and Ceredigion. She is interested in connection with the land, memory, personal history and identity.